LEGENDS

CLARK GABLE

CLARK GABLE

INTRODUCTION BY
JAMES CARD

SERIES EDITOR
JOHN KOBAL

Photographs from
THE KOBAL COLLECTION

Little, Brown and Company
Boston   Toronto

To Joan Crawford whose presence
has illuminated so many movies
with and without Clark Gable
                                    J.K.

19/43028
G 115 C

I would like to thank Ben Carbonetto; Mark Ricci,
Memory Shop; Mary Corliss, Museum of Modern Art; Mark Viera;
and Brian Rule, C.I.S. for their contributions to this book.
                                            John Kobal

Introduction Copyright © 1986 by James Card
Afterword Copyright © 1986 by John Kobal and Laszlo Willinger
Photographs Copyright © 1986 by The Kobal Collection

Library of Congress Catalog Card No. 85–82203

First American Edition

Designed by Craig Dodd

Printed in Italy

CONTENTS

1

CLARK GABLE

There are elusive mysteries about the career of Clark Gable. There are questions that have driven each of his biographers to more speculation than should be expected in describing the life of one of filmdom's most visible and seemingly uncomplicated celebrities.

His very beginning cannot be determined with provable certainty. In both Meadville Pennsylvania and Cadiz Ohio there are official certifications of the birth of Clark Gable on the first day of February, 1901. But if there is documentary doubt about his birthplace, no uncertainty troubles today's citizens of grimy, economically blighted Cadiz whose inhabitants mis-pronounce the name of their town, calling it 'Catas' – as in 'catastrophic'.

On 1 February 1986, some two hundred assembled in unpleasant weather, late in the afternoon, to attend ceremonies dedicating a monument to Clark Gable on the site of a razed building where, according to Cadiz lore, Clark Gable was born to Adeline Hershelman Gable, a frail amateur artist who only nine months after the birth of her only child, died at the age of thirty-one.

The unveiling of the monument to Clark Gable was, of course, accompanied by the inevitable proclamations by local politicians. The chairman of the event read a fine letter from President Ronald Reagan, praising Clark Gable for having volunteered for active duty during the Second World War even though he had been well past the age when hazardous action would have been expected of him. Then there was a United States congressman, a Douglas Applegate who looked amazingly like a young Richard Nixon. Congressman Applegate managed to harangue the restless and shivering crowd with misinformation about the career of the honoree that was remarkable, even for a politician. For some reason, he went out of his way to insist that Gable had never appeared in silent films. (He had been in at least four.)

Saddest aspect of the event was the frequently expressed opinion that establishing the Gable monument in Cadiz would bring tourists streaming to that dismal spot, expending voyagers' dollars in amounts sufficient to help ease the woes of a community that once existed by mining coal – now no longer a much wanted fuel. Cadiz boasts of only one other celebrated son – General George Custer. By the looks of the General Custer Hotel in Cadiz, the fame of the ill-fated Indian fighter has brought no substantial group of his admirers to Cadiz since the Battle of Little Big Horn.

A far more appropriate location for a Gable monument would have been eight miles away in Hopedale Ohio where, from his mother's death until he was sixteen, Clark Gable spent the formative years of his boyhood. It seems incredible that there could be a town more dreary than Cadiz, but Hopedale is hopelessly so. Clinging to steep, eroded hillsides, even today the streets of Hopedale are muddy and unpaved. But the Gable home, built by Clark's father William in 1905, still stands solidly and rather handsomely, one of the three or four dwellings in all Hopedale that are not crumbling, ready to slide down the hillside slopes in desperate disrepair.

A visit to Hopedale gives one a clue as to why Clark Gable, at the very peak of his fabulous career, would describe himself to an interviewer as 'just a lucky slob from Ohio'. Even as a teenager, Gable was fastidious about his dress and his appearance. As a film star, his favorite recreations, duck hunting and fishing, saw Gable outfitted like an ad for Abercrombie and Fitch. Had he any detractors, not one would ever choose the word 'slob' to denigrate Clark Gable. Whether or not he really considered himself just lucky, he could not really have seen himself as a slob. His remark was an apology for not only having emerged from the State of Ohio, but from an Ohio town that could only be characterized as lower Slobovia.

American celebrities had better be born in Philadelphia, Boston, Denver, Montreal or even Toronto – best of all in New York City where the inhabitants consider that city the absolute art and cultural center of the world. Elsewhere in the State of New York is not acceptable. 'Upstate' is a curse word applied by the anointed of Manhattan to an area they feel is more remote and primitive than Dawson City.

Ohio is considered Mid-West (although geographically, it is still part of the Eastern States) and the Mid-West although acknowledged to be 'The Cradle of Presidents', is just not felt to be right as providing background and environment for the development of serious artists. Hence Gable's putting himself down as a 'slob from Ohio'.

Growing up in a ghastly place like Hopedale and somehow achieving the legendary status of Clark Gable is indeed a feat worthy of monumental recognition. And how that feat was accomplished provides even more speculative answers to the mystery of one man's having become a film star absolutely unlike any other before him – or any of his contemporaries.

Rudolph Valentino had affected thousands of women like catnip but men, for the most part, were either cool or outright hostile to his image and usually contemptuous of his uninhibited love-making techniques. John Wayne could count on legions of men who admired the rugged masculinity he projected along with the unwavering challenge he implied to the pacifist liberals of his country. But Wayne seldom became a pin-up for adoring women.

Only Clark Gable achieved the seemingly impossible in enlisting the approval of male film goers while he became the ideal man amongst men or women — women who found his sardonic good humor, often turned against himself, along with his tigerish handsomeness, a combination that brought him almost unbearingly close to fantasy fulfilling perfection.

After considering the mystery of how Hopedale could have fuelled the raw material for so exceptional a human being, one is confronted with an even greater puzzle: what motivated a youth of uninspiring Hopedale to pursue a theatrical career with Gable's obsessive determination? Surely nothing given him by his father — unless it was strong reaction against his father's constant anti-cultural stance.

William Gable was a handsome, rugged oil driller, a wandering wild-catter, hard-drinking, rough living individualist who was always determined to see that his son, 'the Kid', should not develop any 'sissified' traits whatsoever. And a life in the theatre or work in motion pictures William Gable considered no proper occupations for a he-man. William Gable had a brother who actually ran a theatre in Sharon Pennsylvania. But there is no record of young Clark's ever having met his uncle much less of having the experience of attending his uncle's establishment in Pennsylvania. In fact, Hopedale was without a theatre — not even a makeshift movie house. It was many years before one of cinema's most successful players ever saw a movie.

Were there genes from Adeline Hershelman, who tried to paint, in young Clark that militated against his father's steadfast ambition to see that his son remained a brawny hard-hat like himself? Clark's work experiences were surely leading him in that direction. With his father, he worked in oil fields. Alone, he was employed in garages, logging camps and with telephone wire crews. Reluctantly, at the age of sixteen, he had wrestled alongside his father trying to coax a living from the stubborn soil of the farm William

2

Gable had acquired near Ravenna Ohio after he had halted his long wandering separations from his family.

Clark Gable found loving support from his understanding stepmother who had high hopes for a stepson that to her, held much promise for exploits far beyond the depressingly limited horizons of Hopedale. She encouraged him at twelve to go to a music teacher. He learned to play the French horn and by thirteen he was playing in the town band. Growing fast, he reached six feet by the time he was fourteen. Husky and over-size, he still did not become the athlete (or the brawler) his father hoped for; running and shot-putting at the high-school track meets were casual activities that did not enlist his all-out enthusiasm.

More significantly, he did have his first taste of performance as a teenager. The high school in Hopedale could not manage such a luxury as an auditorium. School events were held in the Opera House. There Clark Gable first experienced the often addictive spell of being on stage. He sang a duet with a young lady and whatever the audience thought of his initial performance, his father's reaction was to tease him about his singing – a jokingly-serious reminder that William Gable for the rest of his life inflicted on his son, that his hopes for his offspring did not include the singing of soppy songs before an audience.

Was that 1916 flirtation with performance the planting of the seed that would later develop Clark Gable's unyielding determination to become an actor? If it was, it was never acknowledged by Gable in any of his interviews that sought the beginnings of his later formidable pursuit of a firm place in the world of theatre.

But two years later came the key event that Gable himself cited as the ignition of the constant flame of his foremost infatuation.

Attending high-school in Ravenna Ohio, Gable rebelled against any further struggle with nature in the dirt. Dropping out of school in his third year, he left home and went to nearby Akron Ohio, the rubber city where most of the tires on all the automobiles in the United States are made. The tire factories were struggling to supply the wheels of army vehicles being assembled for America's belated entry in the First World War.

Clark Gable, dining in a cheap restaurant in Akron, struck up a conversation with two actors from the Pauline MacLean Players, a stock company then presenting *The Bird*

3

of Paradise. Gable was invited backstage for the performance. He described it as the most beautiful thing he had ever seen. It was that night, he later insisted that changed his life. He had to become an actor.

But haunting the stage doors of stock companies, sometimes even returning back-stage as a call-boy, brought him no chance to stand before an audience again. Wandering through Oklahoma and Oregon he found a succession of rugged outdoor jobs. Until, at last, he helped his destiny to guide him closer to the theatre by taking an indoor, white collar job in Portland Oregon.

There is an early photograph of teenager Clark Gable with his friends on a return visit to Hopedale. Gable stands next to two girls and another boy; the girls and Gable's buddy are dressed just as one would expect kids in gritty Hopedale to be clad. But Clark Gable wears a snappy hat, a long overcoat and gloves. Come of age in 1922, for once the would-be Beau Brummell takes a job quite unlike anything his father had ever lured him into. He moves indoors and becomes a tie salesman in the Portland Oregon Department Store of Meir and Frank.

'A lucky slob from Ohio who happened to be in the right place at the right time' he told an interviewer. Meir and Frank's was the right place and it was a lucky time to be there for Clark Gable because at the next counter was an at-liberty actor, between shows. The actor was Earle Larimore whose aunt was Laura Hope Crews, an established actress on Broadway who would later enliven Garbo's film *Camille*. Larimore was a member of the Red Lantern Players in Portland, when he wasn't selling men's furnishings and once again Clark Gable became a stage-door johnny – not, certainly, trying to date an actress – but desperately hoping to find himself again on the boards.

When at last that hope was realized, his acting was considered abominable but his presence was ubiquitous and finally he was given a place in the Astoria Stock Company, albeit it was given most begrudgingly. With the memory of his singing role in *The Arrival of Kitty* back in Hopedale at the Opera House, he used part of the small amount he was earning selling ads and working again as a mechanic, to take singing lessons. He even dared taking a job singing in a Portland Hotel.

It was at the age of twenty-two that the stage-struck wanderer from Ohio, not considered handsome at all, appearing clumsy and inept on stage, met the woman who was to bring about the profound change in his life that would amount to a solid preparation for a successful career in the theatre. The woman was actress Josephine Dillon who had appeared in several plays in New York (without particular distinction) and was about to form a theatre group in Portland.

Dillon saw in this gawky young man with wide gaps in his teeth, out-sized hands and phenomenal ears, the magnetic promise of qualities that would later mark him apart from every other actor. Quite literally Josephine Dillon took 'The Kid' (seventeen years her junior) in hand. As a drama coach she worked with his speech and his bearing. She did what she could to improve his appearance. His tiny, spaced-out front teeth were replaced by two normal sized gold ones – to be sure a questionable improvement that required his painting them white whenever he went on stage.

The next year, 1924, Josephine Dillon went to Hollywood founding the Dillon Stock Company and an acting school. Gable followed her to California, took a part in her production of *Miss Lulu Bett* and continued his exhaustive lessons under her guidance – guidance that led him into marriage for the first time. Clark Gable and his mentor and coach were married 18 December, 1924.

As his coach, agent and wife, Josephine Dillon was tireless (according to her own accounts) in preparing her husband for the career that would separate them. Without enthusiasm – he was after a place in the theatre – Gable took a few roles in films that were still without dialogue. The first picture he appeared in, not as an extra, but as one of the credited members of the cast was Louis Gasnier's 1924 film *White Man*. Clark Gable's name was listed in the credits as the brother of the leading lady, Alice Joyce.

His appearance in *The Plastic Age* a Clara Bow vehicle brought about no gasps of excitement (as would the brief appearances of Gary Cooper in the same star's *It* and in *Wings*). Even the predatory eye of Catherine the Great as played by Pola Negri in Lubitsch's *Forbidden Paradise* did not linger with lust on the husky grenadier whose uniform Clark Gable filled out so impressively. Nor did the genius of Erich Stroheim notice in the uniformed extra Gable played in *The Merry Widow* any exceptional promise. Ironically that handsome bit player found himself ignored in the very MGM studio he would dominate for decades, lost among the extras supporting MGM's biggest superstar, John Gilbert – the star Gable would surpass and eclipse in less than ten years.

In fact, Clark Gable was not yet ready for films. He was a reluctant film actor. Whatever hopes Mrs Gable had for him crashing the studio gates were not shared by her husband. His love was directed exclusively toward the theatre and his sole ambition was Broadway. Josephine Dillon always claimed that she promised Clark Gable she would see that he achieved that goal. And to Josephine Dillon, a promise had to be kept.

In the spring of 1925 Clark Gable encountered another in the long line of perceptive women that would fuel his trip to the summit. This time the actress was a famous lady of the Theatre. None other than Jane Cowl. Gable joined her company in Los Angeles as an understudy. Miss Cowl did not have to study Mr Gable long to discover an undeniable charm and appeal that triumphed over gold teeth, outstanding ears and lessening clumsiness. Gable assumed the role of Mercutio when Jane Cowl toured a successful Juliet to Portland, Seattle and Vancouver.

At last Clark Gable was established as a professional actor – even as a Shakespearean actor! Good roles came his way. In *What Price Glory* he played Sergeant Quirt through four months. With another stock company he met another actress who responded appropriately to the Gable magnetism – Pauline Frederick played with him in her famous *Madame X*.

In 1926 he was cast in Lionel Barrymore's memorable production of *The Copperhead*. Barrymore became a firm supporter of Clark Gable. He thought that Clark had the same kind of animal aggressiveness as Jack Dempsey. There was indeed a kind of resemblance to the world-champion heavyweight fighter. Clark Gable had no lofty brow that some women like to think marks a man as being intellectual. Like Dempsey's, Gable's forehead was tigerish.

Ethnically, Clark Gable's own mother and his father were both descended from Dutch and German immigrants. When the Nazis began their depredations and some researchers claimed the Gables had formerly been Goebels, MGM panicked and had their studio publicists invent Irish ancestry for their major star. For this deception the Irish had their revenge. *Parnell* became one of Gable's few film disasters. But Clark with his jet black hair and combative profile probably inherited those features from the same Germanic group of Wendish Goths that gave the world of sport Max Schmeling.

The stage roles being played by Gable often provided him with basic characterizations

4

that he would carry successfully into film roles later on. As a reporter in *Chicago*, a play starring Nancy Carroll, he developed a character he would repeat many times in his films – notably in *It Happened One Night*. It was a portrayal eminently suited to his own personal charisma – cheeky and sardonically humorous – irreverent and with an engagingly cheerful cynicism.

1926 became a crucial year for Clark Gable in that it brought him his first unqualified success in the field of his insistent ambition and his first taste of the adoration of perhaps too many admirers along with celebrity that made him instantly lionized by the public he encountered outside the theatre. All this happened to him in Houston, Texas where he worked with the Houston Stock Company, Palace Theatre. The repertoire offered two new plays every week. When he did Matt Burke in *Anna Christie* he found a role Clark Gable was perfectly equipped to handle just as O'Neill had intended.

Among the many female worshippers Ria Langham, was the daughter of a wealthy Texas socialite. At this point all biographers of Clark Gable tell different stories. Some, ignoring the daughter's interest in Clark Gable, have her mother as one of the owners of the Houston Stock Company, boosting Gable's position. This version even claims her instrumentality in the roles he achieved in Los Angeles.

But his first wife's account is quite different. According to Josephine Dillon, while her husband basked in the warmth of his Texas fans, true to her promise to see that her progressing pupil would eventually make it on Broadway, she was in New York, doggedly selling her husband's talent where it counted most. Her steadfast efforts finally paid off. From Houston, Clark Gable went to New York where he was cast opposite Zita Johann in *Machinal*. His role was as ideal for him as Matt Burke had been. Still painting his gold teeth white, he performed on the stage with complete confidence – and success. The veteran critics of Manhattan praised him as being 'vigorous and brutally masculine'. The actor who shared his dressing room remembered him as being always 'immaculately dressed'. Gable, a slob no more, was able to impress Manhattan with the timbre of his voice and the style of his dress. Ohio was far behind. And as he had discarded his Mid-West accent and every trace of Hopedale, he decided to jettison his wife and faithful teacher. Josephine was instructed to go back West and leave the Conqueror to enjoy the spoils of his victory. The spoils turned out to be Ria Langham,

5

now a rich Texas widow with a luxurious apartment in New York, N.Y.

If there is a greater sin than ingratitude, it is surely expecting gratitude. Josephine Dillon Gable never forgave her former husband. In the coming years he would be hounded by chiding articles. MGM was blackmailed by her demands. It may be that Clark did break her heart. But she did her utmost to make him pay dearly.

Gable and the elegant, fiscally impressive Ria Langham began appearing together in Manhattan's proper places with regularity. It became obvious that his first marriage was evaporating rapidly. After *Machinal*, Gable managed to get three or four roles in lesser vehicles including one from which he had the distinction of being fired by George M. Cohen who replaced Gable with himself.

Between shows, he watched other plays along with Ria. One of them he attended moved him more than anything he'd seen since that crucial Akron production of *The Bird of Paradise*. It was *The Last Mile* in which Spencer Tracy was electrifying audiences as Killer Mears. Perhaps Gable saw that role as a supreme challenge to his ability as a dramatic actor rather than as a dramatic personality.

Meanwhile, he managed to create another biographical mystery. Sometime in 1929 or 1930 he married Ria Langham after supposedly getting a Mexican divorce. It was an alleged event that occurred before Josephine Dillon had obtained her divorce. His last Broadway role, in support of Alice Brady was, ironically enough, *Love Honor And Betray*.

When Gable was offered the role of Killer Mears in the California company of *The Last Mile*, he was at first reluctant to accept. Perhaps the later friendly but profound rivalry that developed between him and Spencer Tracy had its origin in his recognition – with some degree of envy, no doubt – of the power of Tracy's Killer Mears.

Finally he agreed to take the role but his doubts about his ability to match Tracy's performance seemed confirmed when the play opened in San Francisco and closed with no shouts of approval.

But when *The Last Mile* opened in the Belasco Theatre in Los Angeles 7 January, 1930, it was as though it were an entirely different play from the one so coolly received a short distance north. Clark Gable became an instant celebrity as Killer Mears. His triumph on the West Coast brought him the inevitable screen offers from an industry with scouts out for players who could handle the new problem that was all but over-whelming them — dialogue.

The first role he accepted in the talkies was the part of a heavy in a Western to be shot in Arizona. The film starred William Boyd who would keep his chaps and spurs on a long time in later years as Hopalong Cassidy. Before they went on location, Clark Gable took a crash course in riding from a famous wrangler, Art Wilson. Wilson was a fine instructor and Gable, a fast study. His riding in the film looks as though he'd spent years in the saddle.

The March 1931 issue of *Photoplay Magazine* on page 56 reviews MGM's *Dance Fools Dance* starring Joan Crawford. Gable was in the film, his first for MGM since *The Merry Widow*. On page 57 there is also a review of *The Painted Desert* his Western with Bill Boyd. Both reviews are highly favorable; neither one mentions Clark Gable. But Joan Crawford began giving Clark Gable the most favorable reviews. Indeed she never stopped mentioning him favorably throughout the rest of her life.

If Clark as Killer Mears had made an indelible mark with the theatre-going folk of Los Angeles, he still had to intrigue the filmgoing public. When he played the heavy in *Night Nurse*, a film for Warner Brothers, opposite Barbara Stanwyck, he still attracted no frantic following. But his work did catch the infallible eyes of Irving Thalberg at MGM. On 4 December, 1930, Thalberg signed Clark Gable to a contract that guaranteed him $33,800 a year. The theatrical career of Clark Gable was ended. His entry to the world of film had been officially declared.

Under the paternalistic worries of MGM, their new player's status as a possible bigamist had the studio more than uneasy. The moment Josephine Dillon's divorce was final, the studio had Clark Gable and Ria Langham married officially and in California.

Now Clark Gable, actor was ready for his final metamorphosis into MGM star and we arrive at the solution of the final mystery of his career — the answer to the question as to why Clark Gable should have succeeded far beyond the achievements of a Chester Morris, a John Mack Brown, a Neil Hamilton — any of the other actors who were good looking stars with a solid appearance of masculinity.

Gable brought to the studio a rugged handsomeness, and personality traits of male beastliness with a sense of humor, qualities that would define the difference between

6

him and all the other film actors who possessed only some of those attributes. But for the rest, it took the careful grooming of studio experts – the make-up department, the costumers, the portrait specialists like Hurrell, C. S. Bull and above all, the magnificent cinematographers under long term contracts to MGM to turn the stage actor into an historically irresistible movie idol. It was not enough for Clark Gable to have beguiled Jane Cowl, Pauline Frederick, Josephine Dillon and Ria Langham and Adela Rogers St John (who never stopped writing his praises). Clark Gable had to be sold and shown to the film public as the man for whom every woman longs.

There could be no more painted gold teeth; his teeth were capped and ultimately replaced. There could be no more Jack Dempsey-Max Schmeling eyebrows – they had to be shaped. He had to work out constantly in the studio gym to keep his shoulders broad in relationship to a waist-line threatened by a healthy appetite for steak and booze. His reward for such annoyances: by 1931 he had top billing in *Sporting Blood* – really his own picture with no super-star to share the spotlight.

In the 30's the movies were making folk heroes of the prohibition-spawned gangsters. Every suburban American family boasted its private bootlegger to keep wine on the dinner table and gin in the family cocktail-shaker. The criminals who defied the unpopular Federal agents trying in vain to suppress a flow of alcohol were secretly cheered on by the law-unabiding citizens. Gable played more than his share of gangsters and gamblers in films like *The Secret Six, The Finger Points, Laughing Sinners*. And then came the film that brought to Clark Gable an unprecedented dimension.

A Free Soul was a major film for Norma Shearer. The wife of Irving Thalberg rated the finest supporting cast available. The cast included Lionel Barrymore – one of the earliest of the Gable admirers. But, most importantly, there was Leslie Howard.

In the 30's, Leslie Howard became just about every American's notion of what a Briton should be and sound like. Ironic certainly that Leslie Stainer was of Galician descent and his English of a quality that the Professor Higgins he later played, would have detected as scarcely Oxfordian. But even more than being the ultimate Englishman with Americans, for women who fancied they most admired men of intellectual bearing and sensitivity, with gentle, considerate love-making techniques, Leslie Howard represented close to an ideal. He was devoted beyond reason; he was poetic to the point of dying gracefully; his passion was elegantly constrained. He was, they felt, the perfect lover. Until they saw him opposite Clark Gable. They saw what the wayward, emancipated daughter played by Norma Shearer in *A Free Soul* beheld when Clark Gable as the dinner-jacketed, menacing gangster opposed the effete gentleman of Leslie Howard. Gentlemen, they decided – along with Norma Shearer – were nice but *men* like Clark Gable were what they really needed. Ironically, Leslie Howard was doomed once more to provide a target for the firepower of Clark Gable when as Ashley, he faced the machine-gun diction of Rhett Butler.

Being interviewed by David Frost, Joan Crawford once put it perhaps too bluntly. She'd been asked that of all the actors she had worked with, which one was the most exciting. Her reply was 'Clark Gable of course.' Injudiciously, Frost asked why. 'Because he had balls' she answered with candour enough to have the interchange wiped off the air. Later on, she put her opinion in writing, more discreetly. 'This magnetic man had more sheer animal magic than anyone in the world and every woman knew it.' And writing again; 'I don't believe any woman is telling the truth if she ever worked with Gable and did not feel twinges of sexual urge beyond belief, I would call her a liar.' From her first film with him, Crawford claimed she recognized his special power. 'I knew when this man walked on the set and I didn't know which door he came in, but I knew he was there. That's how great he was.'

With the release of *A Free Soul*, Gable's career rocketed. He could have gone on indefinitely playing gangsters and reporters – his career might have resembled that of arch rival and good buddy Spencer Tracy. Only one element was lacking to catapult him to the legendary status he achieved, transforming him from an enormously popular star to a national menace to the peace of mind of thousands of yearning women.

The film that supplied the missing dimension to the Gable charisma was *Men In White*. Without the dashing moustache, dressed in hospital whites and enacting a pre-Code role of surprising frankness, Gable displayed an emotion competely new to his repertoire – compassion.

Here at last was this overwhelmingly virile, handsome creature, established as being almost brutally savage in his treatment of women, behaving with a tenderness that surpassed all the gentleness of Leslie Howard or Jimmy Stewart. His sober concern for

7

the nurse who finds herself pregnant by another Doctor, made Gable's charisma totally complete. Here at last in the illusory imagery of the motion picture was the ideal man – no matter what any woman's ideal of manhood might be – it had to be identical to the persona now bound up in the screen behaviour of Gable.

Many readers of *Gone With the Wind* were certain that Margaret Mitchell had created Rhett Butler deliberately in the unmistakable pattern of Clark Gable. But as Miss Mitchell pointed out herself, when she began describing Rhett Butler on paper, Clark Gable was not on view on motion picture screens though she was still writing when Gable burst forth on the screen.

What she had done in creating Rhett Butler was to construct in words the man every woman dreamed about even as they realized such a one did not exist. To everyone's amazement by the time her book was ready for publication he did exist and there was never any question but that unless Clark Gable played Rhett Butler, there could be no proper film of *Gone With the Wind.*

That *Gone With the Wind* will endure as a classic among motion pictures is uncertain. Had George Cukor remained as its director the chances of its having been a truly great film would have been mightily enhanced. Victor Fleming, good friend that he was of Clark Gable, was a competent director and an efficient one. But he lacked the ability to create the nuances of a Sternberg, or Vidor, Dreyer or Bunuel just as he lacked the epic vision of Abel Gance. Cukor did what he could in secret sessions with the ladies of the cast to evoke from them quality beyond the cardboard stereotypes that the scenario invited. There is a story one hopes is untrue, that Gable insisted on having Selznick replace George Cukor with Victor Fleming. Supposedly Gable was put off by Cukor's homosexuality. The story is not quite credible in that Cukor never exhibited overt traits of gaiety that could be calculated to upset super he-man Gable. Nor does the myth resemble any of the usual reactions of Gable who was not known for interfering with managerial authority for whatever reasons. And there is no hint of such meddling interference by Gable in Irene Mayer Selznick's account of the problems surrounding the making of *Gone With the Wind* though she does not suggest any reason for her husband's firing their good friend George Cukor in favor of Victor Fleming. The substitution remains a mystery. Two reasons might account for the shift. One was Gable's admiration of Victor Fleming who had already directed him with great success in *Red Dust*, *The White Sister*, and *Test Pilot* – roles that helped to shape and define the Gable personae, and, two, Fleming had a recognised flair for the epic without losing the human interest with films like *Treasure Island*, and *Captains Courageous* – and while Cukor was renowned as a woman's director, Selznick did not want *Gone With the Wind* to become a 'woman's' picture.

Gable took on the role of Fletcher Christian with the same reluctance that later he accepted Rhett Butler and in both cases those films along with *Red Dust* and *It Happened One Night* are likely to be the films for which Clark Gable will be best remembered.

It was in 1960 that Gable remarked to reporter Bill Davidson, 'You know this King stuff is pure bullshit.' The 'King stuff' began in 1938 – a year in which only two Gable films were released. It was the result of a newspaper poll conducted by Ed Sullivan, then a columnist on the *New York Daily News*. The contest involved having readers vote for the 'King and Queen of Hollywood'. There were twenty thousand votes that elected Clark Gable King and Myrna Loy as Queen. This was only a year after Gable's critical flop – *Parnell* – with Queen-to-Be Myrna Loy as his leading lady. And his coronation took place before *Gone With the Wind* so completely confirmed it – and re-confirmed it every time *Gone With the Wind* was revived over the years.

The Gable marriages have figured largely in the several biographies that have been attempted. Sometimes these works have been essayed by those who knew him well – his last wife, Kay Spreckels and his long-time secretary-business manager, Jean Garceau. At other times by those who never met him. These biographies never agree on rather basic points of his personal life. Did his first wife who admittedly coached and schooled him in acting technique really get him started on a Broadway theatrical career only to have him reject her completely the moment he had the lead in Arthur Hopkins' *Machinal*? She has made that claim. Or did Ria Langham arrange to have him given the role after his successful appearance in Houston as Matt in *Anna Christie*? There have been many suggestions that Gable used these two women as 'stepping stone marriages' and abandoned both the moment he achieved his goals.

A woman rejected is capable of any calumny and if the discarded ladies' accusations are true, then Clark Gable in his maturity must have done the most complete shift of character since Mr Hyde returned to being Dr Jekyll. Whatever the truth, Gable in his interviews never complained about either of his former wives, never tried to justify his leaving them, never posed for aggrieved images.

But all who knew Clark Gable and Carole Lombard agreed that with her he finally found the most completely suitable mate. With Lombard he no longer sought the mother which some psychologists claim he kept seeking in adulthood after the deprivation he suffered in the first year of his life. They point to the older women he married and the fact that he even called the younger Lombard 'Ma'.

Gable had learned stagecraft, diction and poise from wife Josephine Dillon. From Ria Langham he learned to move in wealthy social circles without clumsiness or embarrassment – for he was insecure – not only as a high school drop-out, but as an emigrant from seamy Hopedale and the son of a father who never stopped expressing his contempt for Clark's theatrical career. 'Kid, give up this silly acting and do a man's work, advised his father after Clark had bought him a comfortable home not far from Clark's own ranch – after his 'silly business' had netted him a fabulous income.

But with Carole Lombard, he found a beautiful girl – a dropout like himself – a woman who knew and spoke the language of the oil-drillers, the lumberjacks and the garage mechanics her husband had worked with. Happily at ease with Carole, the newly-anointed King chose, not his newspaper poll Queen, Myrna Loy, but rough and ready Carole Lombard to share his throne.

They were married in the spring of 1939 and it was Mrs Carole Lombard Gable who accompanied him to the resplendent premieres of *Gone With the Wind*.

His great love became a casualty of the Second World War, hurrying home to her husband on a plane she was not supposed to take, after a record-breaking bond tour.

Stunned with surely the deepest grief he had ever felt, Gable enlisted in the Air Corps. The move was widely suspected of being a publicity stunt – but only by cynical newsmen who did not know him. Gable was shaven and shorn and at the age of forty-one, as a Private, he did his basic training with inductees who were mostly eighteen, nineteen or twenty. The physical part of his officer's training course gave him no problems. But technical material to learn was tough for one unschooled beyond the tenth grade. But

8

he made it after heroic efforts of memory cramming harking back to his Houston Texas stock company days when they were doing two plays a week.

Overseas, his fellow officers realized quite soon that Captain Gable was not participating in a studio-inspired make-believe. Armed with a 16mm Cine-Special, Captain Gable flew five missions over Germany with a price on his head offered by Goering and special instructions from Adolf Hitler who collected Gable films and longed to have the actor in person on hand – dead or alive. German gunners came close to accommodating him – they shot the heel off his boot on one of his five missions.

In 1944 Major Gable returned to Los Angeles to see to the editing of the footage he'd produced. On 12 June he was discharged with honors, by Captain Ronald Reagan.

For Clark Gable, civilian, the post-war period was bad and bleak. Although MGM was then paying him $7,500 a week, he was doing nothing to earn it. His first film after his return was released in 1945. *Adventure* with Greer Garson was his first failure since *Parnell*. He began a period of high living, hard drinking and low depressions.

For years Gable had a special entourage of extra-marital women friends – some of them appearing again and again – always available when he wanted them. Others were glamorous models and socialites. Among his regulars were Virginia Grey, Carol Gibson, Gwen Seeger. There were prominent beauties: Anita Colby and Millicent Rogers. And he was always a welcome caller at Joan Crawford's. It was a period when he became a hard-riding motorcyclist with a group of close, disaster-seeking friends.

And then he made a big mistake. There are many theories about his choice of Sylvia Ashley as his next bride. One writer supposes that he saw in her another Lombard for she was blonde, witty and effervescent and notwithstanding her marriages to no fewer than two British aristocrats, she had been a rough and tumble performer in vaudeville and night clubs, and her previous husband was Douglas Fairbanks Sr, a king in his own day.

But if her beginning had been theatrical, her life style was intended to reflect the name she bore as Lady Ashley.

There had been an earlier period in Hollywood when many members of what was considered Hollywood Royalty sought to confirm their illustrious status by marriages to genuine European titles. Gloria Swanson, Pola Negri, Constance Bennett and many others swanked about as Marquises, Countesses and Duchesses. What Anglophile Douglas Fairbanks thought he might acquire by marrying Lady Ashley thereby abandoning the established matriarch of Hollywood, Mary Pickford, is difficult to imagine. But marry her he did and revelled in a union that brought him as a frequent visitor to the estates of the likes of the Duke of Sutherland and other Lords of the Empire.

Did Gable think to class up his Hopedale beginnings by acquiring a Lady Ashley? Whatever his reasons, the marriage turned out to be a ghastly mistake. Sylvia redecorated his beloved home with taste more redolent of music halls than the estates of British nobility. Though she made a valiant attempt to follow her husband on his duck-shooting, fishing expeditions, her embarrassing imposition of flouncy decor around rugged cabins became a huge annoyance to her unhappy husband.

After a disastrous dinner party that pained Gable to the point of leaving his guests and hiding in his room, he had enough. Once again, the charge of heartlessness could be laid at his door as he ended his marriage with little ceremony but impressive settlement.

Threading through the multitudinous affairs and impermanent attachments of Clark Gable, one begins to wonder. Here was a man pursued to the point of harassment by literally thousands of adoring women. Without glancing back at them, he engaged in his own pursuit of seemingly countless females, many of them so much older than himself many so moderately attractive that his closest friends began to wonder what it was with him.

Could he have been actually a victim of Don Juanism, beset by insecurities that drove him to seek out women who would expect nothing from him but be profoundly grateful for whatever he was willing or able to give them?

In spite of the constant and glowing testimonials of Miss Crawford, there were cited some episodes of sexual embarrassment that may or may not have had foundation in fact. But the idea is ironic: Clark Gable, the absolute embodiment of sensual virility, longed for and physically hunted by hundreds of hungry women while he himself rushed about in a search for undemanding, impermanent attachments.

In his last marriage, he found a lovely woman who did not shrink from becoming to him, as much as one possibly could, a substitute Carole Lombard. Everything she did,

9

she did for Clark. She shot ducks and caught fish. She roughed it in his favorite places and did not paint the rooms of his home in shocking pink. She came to him with a ready-made family – two children he enjoyed – and best of all – she bore him a son – albeit too late. He died before his son was born.

But to delve about in the insoluble mysteries of Clark Gable's private life is wholly irrelevant. For the medium of motion pictures is one of illusion. It consists of shadows of images that don't even really move – we only imagine them moving. It is all fantasy and magic – trickery of the optic nerve and emotion that lingers in the central nervous system. Our response to film is akin to our emotional enjoyment of music. And the echoing and re-echoing contribution of Clark Gable is that his shadow on the screen is able to evoke the most overpowering – the most vibrant and sensual of all our dreams of splendid manhood.

In this day of the microchip and computer, there are those who have written confidently that given the right programming, a computer will be able to construct a sure-fire block-buster, a multi-million dollar grossing film script. Maybe so. But that computerized Academy Award winning script may yet appear. What we can be sure will not appear in human form or in any robotized replicant, is Clark Gable – he was unique to our own time.

JAMES CARD

11

12

13

14

15

17

19

21

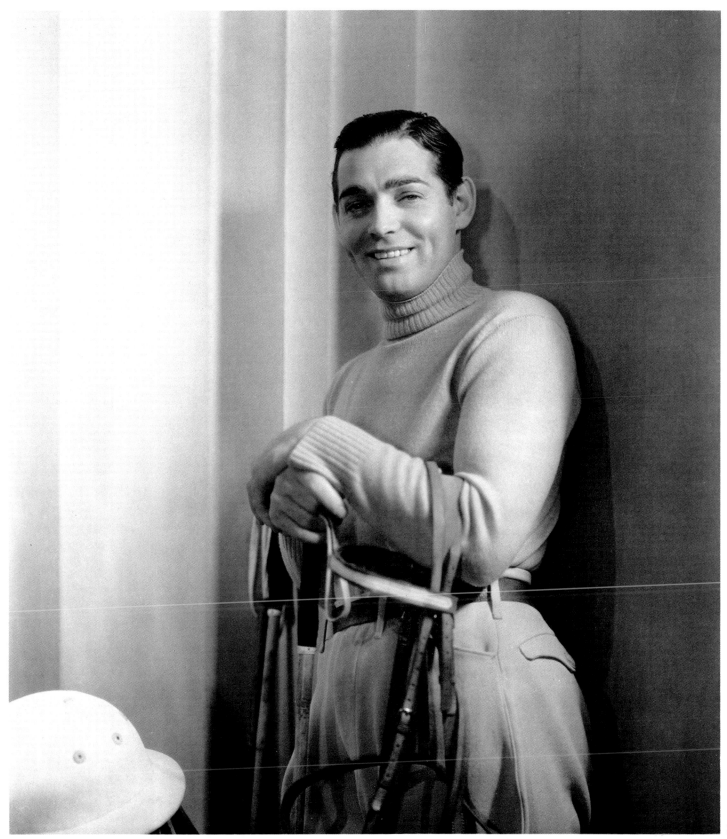

23

24

26

27

29

31

'Why do you throw $500 of our money on a test for that big ape? Didn't you see those big ears when you talked to him? And those big feet and hands, not to mention that ugly face of his?'

Jack Warner
reacting to Clark Gable's screen test, 1930

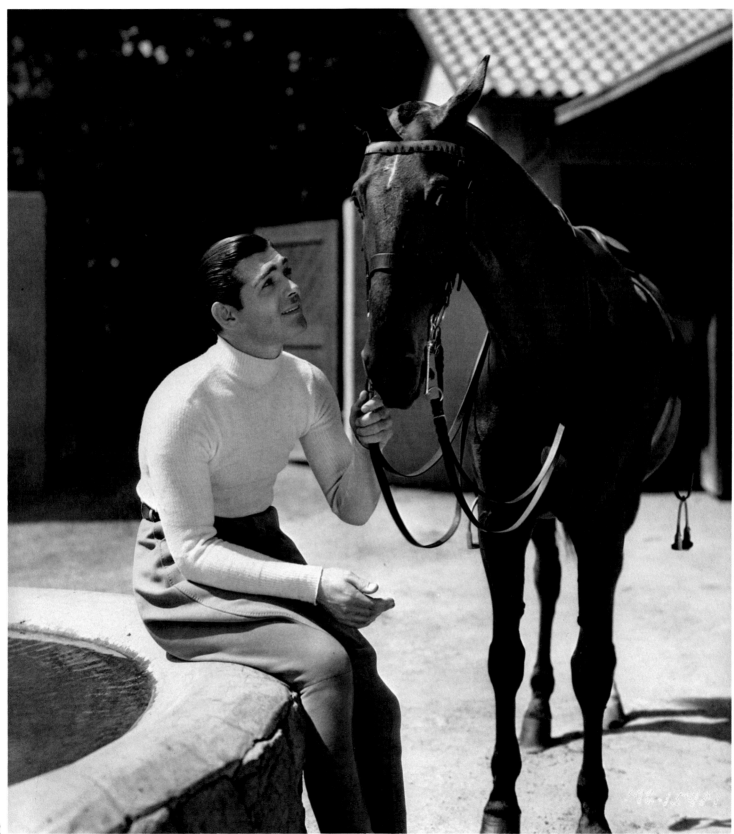

MG-31786

33

34

36

37

38

40

'A lumberjack in evening clothes, the answer to 10 million maidens' prayers, a big kid playing with fireworks, wants to quit work while young and travel, hates wing collars and patent leather shoes, never wears buttonaires, golfs and swims, wears old sweaters and flannel trousers, smokes a pipe and needs a new one, born lazy and admits it, six-foot-one and all muscle, weighs almost 200 pounds in the bathtub, thinks he ought to duck stardom, likes his steaks rare. (He would!) Likes to write left-handed but isn't. 'How'm I doing?' his favourite greeting. Hides behind the set when powdering his make-up, shaves himself with a straight razor and always nicks his chin, hasn't gotten over blushing, especially enjoyed working with Garbo, would like a million dollars.'

Screenland, January 1932

41

'A star in the making has been made. A star that, to our reckoning, will outdraw every other star pictures has developed. Never have we seen audiences work themselves into such enthusiasm as when Gable walks on the screen.'

The Hollywood Reporter, 1931

42

43

44

45

46

47

'Up on the screen, he was a buffalo type who would bust through doors, but innately he was a gentleman — kind, thoughtful and tender . . . Inside he was a gentle man in every sense of the word.'

Delmer Daves,
director of *Never Let Me Go,* 1953

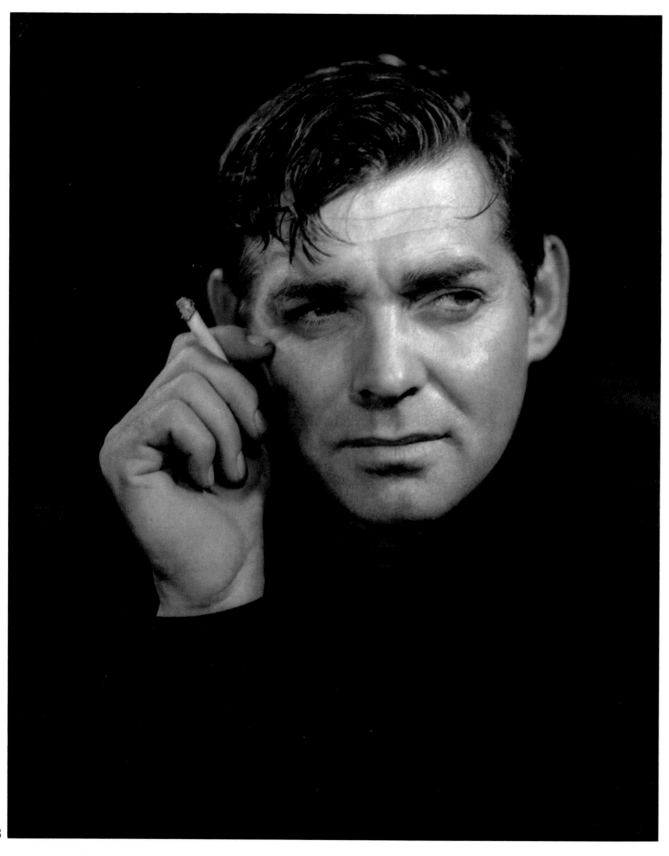

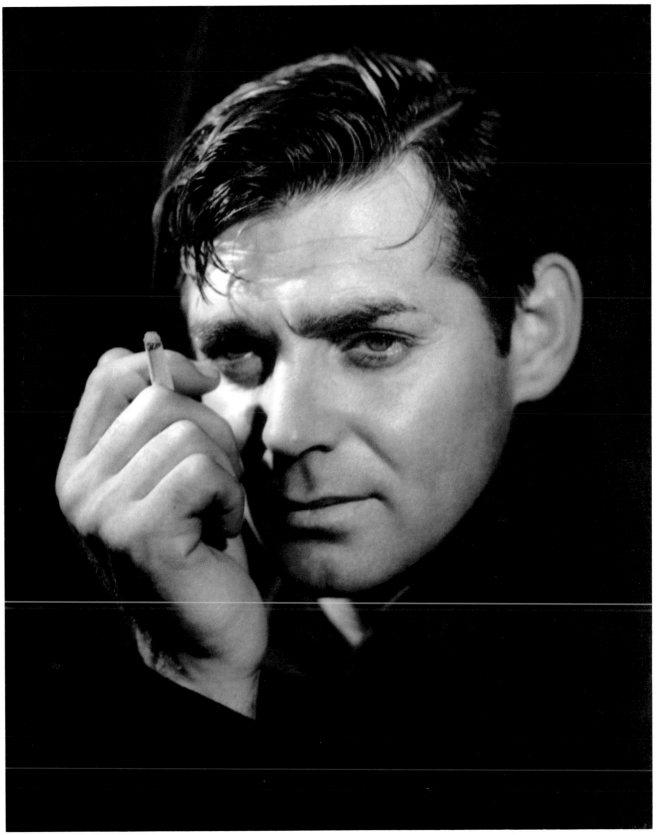

'During the year I've been in films I have been in twelve pictures. I have played a cowboy, a milkman, a chauffeur, several gangsters, a newspaper reporter, a marine aviator, a plain bum, practically everything.

And during these months I have grown to like pictures. Today I think of nothing else. I am afraid of rapid success. It is so easy to stick a pin in a balloon. It worries me. I have been broke too often, broke and stranded, I have seen my hopes built up and dashed down too often, to have any illusions of quick success.'

Clark Gable, 1931

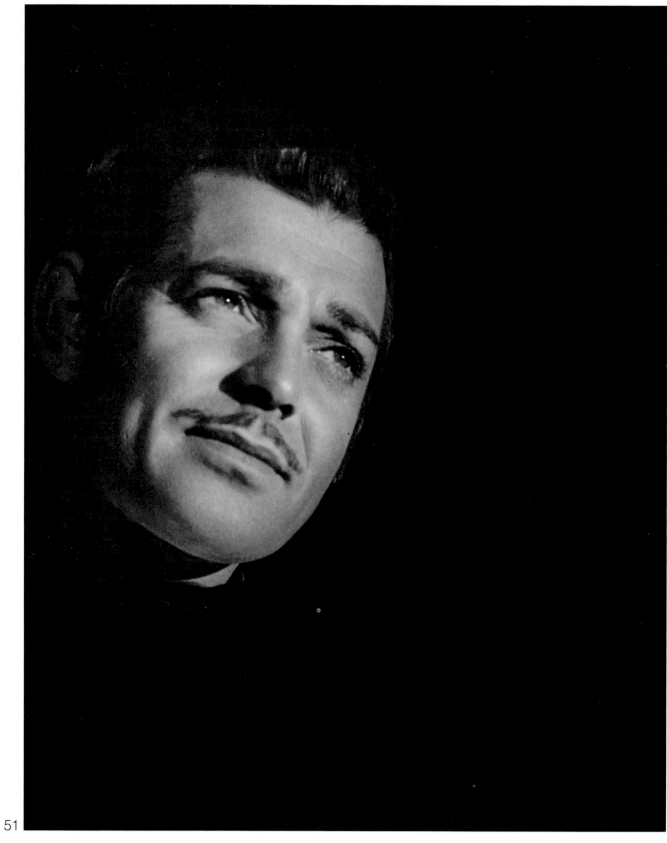

51

54

55

'My God you're big!'

Joan Crawford

56

57

59

'. . . He radiated such charm and vitality that I
began to see what people meant when they said a
sort of magic happened when he was present.
When he smiled his crooked smile he seemed
much handsomer than he was on the screen.'

Jean Garceau
(Gable's personal secretary)

'There is no use trying to explain Clark Gable. He simply possesses, through the strange and fantastic medium of the camera, a dynamic and glittering force. Seen through the magic lens, he has that peculiar power to stimulate emotions in those who watch him, which is the one unfailing uniform characteristic of the few idols the screen has known.'

Adela Rogers St. John, 1932

'Gable made villains popular. Instead of the audience wanting the good man to get the girl, they began wanting the bad man to get her.'

Norma Shearer

64

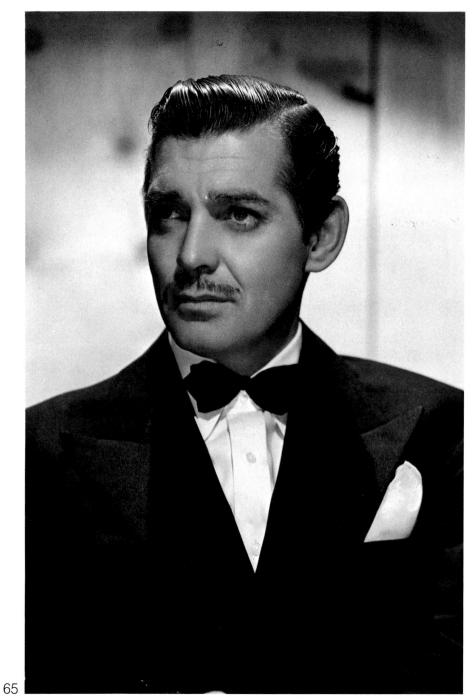

66

68

69

'I had never met Clark, and like every woman in the country, thought he was divine. I also jumped at the gay prospect of looking at him every day — and getting paid besides!'

Claudette Colbert,
after *It Happened One Night,* 1934

72

73

'I know I haven't fooled the public with these dinner-jacket parts I've been playing for the past year or more. What's more, I don't like to fool them even if I could. I'd like to get back to Gable the roughneck and forget Gable the gentleman. I guess what I really want more than anything else is a chance to be myself again, both on and off the screen.'

Clark Gable, 1934

78

'When I was growing up, Clark Gable represented everything I idealised . . . and to find that ideal was all I ever dreamed of, plus so much more – more human, warmer! I am sorry he didn't always receive the recognition for his acting that he deserved, because he cared so very much.'

Marilyn Monroe

80

81

82

'I've never been able to connect stars with parts I write, but after meeting Gable I could see him as Gay Langland (*The Misfits*). He had the same sort of lyricism underneath, something one didn't usually think of, watching him. It was his secret charm – tough but responsive to feeling and ideals.'

Arthur Miller

83

85

86

87

89

90

92

93

'Rare human qualities Mr. Gable possessed in an unusual degree: virility graced by humour, good nature adorned by comprehension, an easy manner unspoiled by pretensions. To these engaging traits he added professional integrity and personal sincerity not easily found in the competitive atmosphere of the screen.'

Editorial, *Los Angeles Times,*
on Gable's death

THE FILM STAR AS PHOTOGRAPHIC MODEL

Laszlo Willinger arrived in Hollywood in the summer of 1937 to work at M-G-M as the head of their portrait department. The stars, especially the great women stars like Joan Crawford, Norma Shearer, and Jean Harlow had been used to, and spoiled by, George Hurrell's brilliant portraits during that celebrated photographer's tenure at Metro. After he stormed out of there in 1932, they kept insisting on him despite the studio's other gallery photographers, like Clarence Sinclair Bull. Bull pleased Greta Garbo, who liked his quiet, reserved, discreetly professional approach to work, but the others did not all feel as secure or as disinterested in the necessary art of self-promotion and felt that only Hurrell could do them justice. This proved both extremely expensive to the studio as his free-lance price rose into the thousands but also deeply humiliating to the publicity department that had allowed him to get away. For the next five years they kept trying to find a photographer whose work would please their demanding stable of stars, and who would also be under contract to them.

Part of the problem was solved when Jean Harlow liked the work of one young local photographer, Ted Allan, and he became her photographer for the last few years of her brief life. But it was with the advent of the Austro-Hungarian photographer Laszlo Willinger that the others capitulated. Norma Shearer adored what he did for her, so did Crawford, and the less demanding but equally professional Myrna Loy. The great male stars under contract, Clark Gable, Spencer Tracy, Nelson Eddy, Robert Taylor, Fred Astaire . . . were somewhat less fussy, or professed to be, but they too relaxed and opened up with Willinger. Later on, when such stars as Hedy Lamarr, Louise Rainer, Greer Garson and Vivien Leigh, as well as such starlets groomed for stardom like Lana Turner, Lucille Ball and others joined, Laszlo did some of their most memorable sessions.

His photographs gave them an aura of allure coupled with intelligence, and, a charming surprising quality of modesty about these otherwise remote creatures: as if they too realized that there was a world out there besides the high paid one of make-believe they inhabited, and in their bearing before his camera they seemed to convey that awareness without losing their attractive larger than life quality: Crawford seemed to become reflective, Norma Shearer had a touch of spring about her; Myrna Loy had a living-room smile and the bedroom in her eyes was now a special glint for just the right man. Willinger's Vivien Leigh portraits for *Waterloo Bridge* and *Gone With the Wind* captured better than any photographs of her before or after, the moment when stardom hits, before it pales, and when forever after, on seeing these portraits he took of her, one can see and say, that is why Vivien Leigh was a sensation. There is a secret and a difference, a surprise and a bold defiance of what tomorrow might bring. No wonder that the unwilling star asked Laszlo to come to San Francisco where she was playing Juliet to Olivier's Romeo and ask him to take their special portraits.

But Laszlo's success was not just in capturing the women stars. In fact, some of his finest work is of men and possibly the best of all are his portraits of the decade's most lionized, idolized star, Clark Gable. Every star has that moment when everything he/she was going to be meets up and forever defines his/her appeal. The portraits Laszlo took of Gable capture both that moment and that appeal. These portraits show Gable as a man in the prime of his life and on top of the world. There is still a touch of the cruelly handsome and slightly dangerous Lothario – in which guise Gable first cracked across the screen (after discouraging years of hanging around one should add) when he co-starred as a night-club owning gangster in the Joan Crawford film, *Dance Fools Dance* and as the man who smacked ladylike Norma Shearer around in *A Free Soul*. But in these Willinger sessions, the brutish caveman is now concentrated in an engaging twinkle in the eyes as well as by that forever roguish smile and the slight sense one gets of tension in the brows above the eye. A lot had happened since those two early 1930/31 films.

Initially, Gable's brute male approach had helped revolutionise America's idea of the romantic lover. With the advent of actors like Gable and Cagney gone were the discreet, gentlemanly lovers of silent films. Everything about Gable was direct, straight on, even his eyes and his crooked clean shaven smile were two fisted. He was a man who would not be buried by the depression – his looks were not for dreaming, or so one would believe from the roughing up he gave his leading ladies as easily as he could punch his way out of a gang of men.

By 1937 and Willinger, his brand of appeal had been broadened, refined, made more accessible so that when the gangster era was over, he would not fall by the wayside the way others do when the tide of fashion turns. Not that there was any need to worry. Audiences liked to see him in anything whether comedy, drama, romantic soap-operas, adventure . . . the lot.

Willinger arrived at Metro at the precise moment when the definitive Gable image clicked in. The photos that came out of their sessions in the gallery are as definitive in their way of who Gable was, what he meant, and why he should have lasted so long and survived so many changes, as in their way, Hurrell's surrealistic portraits of Jean Harlow or Bachrach's extravagant portraits of the coltish Kate Hepburn, and all the other great, timeless sessions to come out of the 50 years of Hollywood's role in providing us with role models. Willinger brings us this Gable, cocky but nice, self-assured but endearing. Gable is playing with the camera, he is putting on that endearing look; he is very confident with his facial expressions; all the more surprising since at the outset of his career, one of his major drawbacks when looking for work was the fact that his ears were not only large but stood out and would have to be taped back, and he knew, even if his public didn't, that his gleaming white teeth were false. Here is a man who doesn't feel his appeal rests on his appearance and that is what makes his appearance so appealing. From these Willinger portraits, the first ones taken three years before he was signed to play Rhett in *Gone With The Wind*, it become apparent why his casting was a foregone conclusion, why in fact the book's author, Margaret Mitchell, confided that when she was writing the book, she had Gable in mind as the prototype for her fictional hero.

These portraits belong to Gable's best work. This is how we remember him and how he remained for the rest of his life, older, wiser but still that same cocky, endearing Gable – a man who had learned to live with being a legend.

JOHN KOBAL

ON PHOTOGRAPHING CLARK GABLE

Gable had something extremely rare, he looked good from any angle. Most people have a good and bad side, best from one angle only. He could be photographed under any lighting conditions, any camera angle. There was another, probably more important factor. He was the least self-conscious person in front of the camera. Myrna Loy was like Gable in this respect. She seemed to be at ease with herself and saw posing for stills as another part of her profession, which she took seriously. As I said in the past, professionals can smell each other and are comfortable with each other and she certainly respected me as a fellow professional. And then, on the other end of the scale, there was Marilyn Monroe whose whole life revolved around the camera. She only came to life when she saw that glass eye pointed at her. Basically, she was a dilettante who always feared that she might be found out. But the camera was safe; it avoided the need of her dealing with real people on a one-to-one basis. As she told me once when I marvelled at her ability to go in a fraction of a second from next to nothing to a lifelike imitation of sparkling vivacity only to drop into dull mediocrity after she heard the click of the camera, 'This is like being screwed by a hundred guys and you can't get pregnant!' Well, Gable simply took it for granted that the man behind the camera was as professional as he was and that both worked for the same purpose, to make him look as appealing as possible.

Most stars, even men, insisted on seeing proofs of all photos taken and they made their own selection of what they permitted to be published. They interfered with the lighting, even the backgrounds, and were deeply concerned with what should be retouched. They even insisted that all original negatives rejected by them be destroyed. Joan Crawford and Norma Shearer to mention two who had that privilege and who exercised it and, of all people, Nelson Eddy. When casting began for *Gone With The Wind*, Gable showed up at my studio in a Confederate uniform, with a sideburn and a moustache and said, 'I want you to shoot some pictures of me in this get-up.' Rather intrigued, I asked him why he wanted these pictures and without smiling he said, 'Don't you see, I AM Rhett Butler.' Those negs were destroyed by our common decision before anyone else ever saw them . . . Gable was sure enough of himself never to bother with such details.

I once talked to him about his easygoing attitude and he said, 'I am getting paid to be in front of the camera and you are getting paid to be behind it and the bosses seem to be satisfied with both of us, so why worry?' He liked his pictures and said so, but it was no great thing for him, or for that matter, for me. Of course, we talked while I was shooting, but mostly it was chit-chat. He was not interested in the mechanics of photography. He simply assumed that I knew my business. He never asked me to photograph his wife, nor did he, to my knowledge, ever ask for any special prints and certainly not to give as gifts to anybody. He was not vain or so presumptuous as to give pictures of himself as gifts. Gable had two distinctly different personalities. When he appeared at official functions, he was the quintessential movie star; he could make an entrance into a room worthy of a Barrymore. He was adept at talking to the press by making the least important cub reporter feel as though he had just got the scoop of the century. To him this was part of the performance for which he was paid. And then there was the other Gable. He was most comfortable away from Hollywood, fishing, hunting . . . mostly with people who had never been in a gossip column. He was given to corny practical jokes. Once, when he was married to Carole Lombard, he gave her as a birthday gift a big ham, adorned with a pink bow. Another time he bought an old rusty jallopy and, without changing its exterior, put a high-performance motor in it just to enjoy the thrill of taking off at 60 miles from a standing start to the amazement of all other drivers on the road. And after work he was often seen sitting around a less than elegant bar across the street from the studio with his cronies . . . electricians, grips, carpenters . . . having a wonderful time being just one of the boys.

He was a man who got what he wanted, never raising his voice and never making enemies . . . indeed a rare exception in Hollywood – then and now – where posturing and self-congratulation are thought to be essential tools of the trade.

When I had to photograph Gable with someone else, for example, when we had to do publicity photographs of the stars which could be used for poster art, Gable didn't demand any prerogative. When I shot him and Joan Crawford for *Strange Cargo* Crawford had to be lighted carefully, Gable got the leak light from the spot on her. At the time I was told they had a short-lived affair, but I have no first-hand knowledge. It certainly wasn't apparent in the way they worked. From what his occasional girls rather indiscreetly conveyed to one and all, he was no great shakes in bed and I am convinced that all Crawford needed for sexual rapture was a mirror. It wasn't lighting he was worried about, just a professional attitude when it came to work. When I was doing the two shots of him with Norma Shearer for *Idiot's Delight* I had the distinct feeling that Gable did not particularly care for her, especially because she kept him (and everybody else) waiting for hours until she made her regal entry on the set and then . . . did not know her lines. He became visibly annoyed when she dithered with her make-up, her hair, her dress etc. when he had been ready for an hour.

There was no difference in my approach to shooting in Hollywood, Paris, Berlin or Vienna. Hollywood was easier for me because the crews were immeasurably more competent. And, of course, sets were built especially according to my instructions, something unheard of in Europe. Everything was made easy in Hollywood . . . as long as the results were good.

As for cameras, lights etc that we used at MGM when I first got there: the standard camera was an 8 × 10 view camera with 12 to 15 inch lenses. Even the photographers on the set used this unwieldy monster. There was no candid camera used in the studios other than a heavy 5 × 7 Graflex which sounded like a pistol shot when it took the exposure. Not until *Life* and *Look* sent their photographers with the 35 mm cameras was there any change . . . and that came very slowly. On the set the photographer, using the lighting of the motion picture first, the camera man rushed into the set with his big camera and recreated a particular moment of the scene by posing the actors. Directors hated them; it took valuable time from their shooting.

One reason for using large format film was that it could be retouched; everything was retouched before the prints were made. Also, the hundreds of prints sent out every day were contact prints . . . the same size as the negative. This made it possible to make prints in a much quicker progression than by putting the negs into the enlarger and blowing them up to 8 × 10.

While I also used 8 × 10 film, I insisted that I make master prints myself through an enlarger. This gave me the luxury of composing as I wanted and to intensify or reduce certain portions of the image according to my idea of what the finished product should look like. Then a dupe neg was made from my master print and that was then used to make contact prints on which my corrections were incorporated . . . permanently.

For lights I used primary spotlights. They are lights with lenses which allowed me literally to paint with light, putting emphasis on certain areas, pinpointing what I considered the most flattering or important area of the composition while leaving unimportant areas in the shade. This was even more dramatic through my making the master print.

Today's system of throwing an overall flat light over everything, washing out all shadows and shooting with motorized cameras and hoping that out of a hundred frames one might get one good one is the exact opposite of what I did. I tried to make a photograph as dramatic as possible by lighting dramatically. That is impossible with today's lighting. Now the photographer is totally dependent on the absolute perfection of his model. Today the model is far more important than the photographer; this, no doubt is the reason that models have become stars in their own right. And quite rightly so. Today's photographer is an observer rather than a creator. He photographs what there is; I photographed what there ought to be. Of course, Clark Gable brought a lot of what there ought to be with him.

LASZLO WILLINGER

THE PHOTOGRAPHS

79 At home 1951, photograph by Eric Carpenter
80 *Across The Wide Missouri* 1951, photograph by Eric Carpenter, MGM
81 *Across The Wide Missouri* 1951, MGM
82 *Never Let Me Go* 1953, off set, MGM
83 *Red Dust* 1932, with Jean Harlow, MGM
84 *Mogambo* 1953, with Ava Gardner, MGM

85 *Red Dust* 1932, off set, MGM
86 *Mogambo* 1953
87 *Mogambo* 1953, with Ava Gardner, off set, MGM
88 *The Tall Man* 1955, with Jane Russell, off set, 20th Century Fox
89 *The Tall Man* 1955, photograph by Frank Powolny, 20th Century Fox

90 *The Tall Man* 1955, photograph by Frank Powolny, 20th Century Fox
91 *The Misfits* 1961, United Artists
92 *The Misfits* 1961, United Artists
93 *The Misfits* 1961, United Artists
94 *The Misfits* 1961, with Marilyn Monroe, United Artists
95 Photograph by John Engstead, 1947